MINI
MONSTERS

Camilla de la Bédoyère

QEB

QEB Publishing

Created for QEB Publishing by Tall Tree Ltd
www.talltreebooks.co.uk
Editors: Jon Richards and Rob Colson
Designer: Jonathan Vipond
Illustration pp18–19:
Mick Posen/www.the-art-agency.co.uk

Copyright © QEB Publishing, Inc. 2012

Published in the United States by
QEB Publishing, Inc.
3 Wrigley, Suite A
Irvine, CA 92618

www.qed-publishing.co.uk

A CIP record for this book is available from the
Library of Congress.

ISBN 978 1 60992 283 2

Printed in China

Picture credits
(t=top, b=bottom, l=left, r=right, c=center, fc=front cover,
bc=back cover)
Alamy 24 Naturepix, 26-27 Phil Degginger, 28bl William
Mullins; **FLPA** bctl Thomas Marent/Minden Pictures, bcb
Christian Ziegler/Minden Pictures, 4–5 Chien Lee, 10bl
Piotr Naskrecki, 28–29 Thomas Marent, 29t Thomas
Marent; **Getty Images** 17 Mark Moffett, 25t Dorling
Kindersley, 26bl James H Robinson, 30 Mark Moffett, 31r
Visuals Unlimited, Inc/Alex Wild; **Nature Picture Library**
3 Rod Williams, 11 Rod Williams, 22–23 Martin Dohrn;
NHPA fc Daniel Heuclin, bctr James Carmichael Jr, 1 John
Cancalosi, 4bl ANT Photo Library, 13 Ken Griffiths, 14–15
ANT Photo Library, 15b Ken Griffiths, 25b John Bell,
30-31 Dave Pinson, 33 John Bell; **Shutterstock** 2–3
Rudchenko Liliia; **SPL** 6b Simon D Pollard, 6–7 Barbara
Strnadova, 7c James H Robinson, 8–9 Solvin Zankl, 9b
Theirry Berrod, Mona Lisa Production, 16 Sinclair
Stammers, 20br Steve Gschmeissner, 20–21 Nature's
Images, 22bl Susumu Nishinaga; **Minibeast Wildlife** 12bl
Alan Henderson; **Creative Commons** 14bl Bjorn Christian
Torrissen.

Web site information is correct at time of going to press.
However, the publishers cannot accept liability for any
information or links found on any Internet sites,
including third-party web sites.

Words in **bold** are explained
in the Glossary on page 32.

HOW
SCARY?

Look for this rating.
It will tell you how
scary and dangerous
each mini monster is.

1—a little scary

2—pretty scary

3—scary

4—QUICK! RUN AWAY!

5—YIKES! TOO LATE!

CONTENTS

Up-close

Check out this
assassin bug
on page 10

SCUTIGERA

Creepy-crawlies, spiders, scorpions, and stinging bugs are some of the world's most incredible creatures. They belong to one enormous group of animals, called **invertebrates**.

BUG BITES

Length: 4 in. (10 cm)

Habitat: Dark, damp places

Where: Mostly in tropical regions

Weapons: Powerful, venom-injecting claws

HOW **SCARY?**

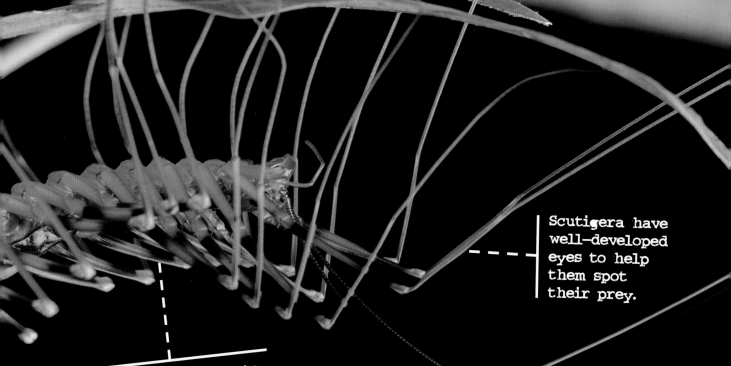

Scutigera have well-developed eyes to help them spot their prey.

Scutigera have up to 15 pairs of long legs, which let them run really fast.

Invertebrates are usually small and they don't have bones, but many of them are still fearsome **predators**. This is a giant long-legged centipede called a scutigera. Its body is divided into parts called **segments**, and there is a pair of legs on most segments.

The first pair of legs has claws that can inject a deadly **venom** into a victim. Scutigera feed on other invertebrates, such as beetles.

KILLER FACT

The venom from some scutigera centipedes is strong enough to make a human very sick.

Creepy Legs

Why does any bug need 15 pairs of legs? They aren't just for running—these limbs have another important job to do. This centipede uses its legs to feel its way in the dark, and to find **prey**.

BIRD-EATING SPIDER

This is no mini monster—it's a maxi monster! The goliath bird-eating spider is the heaviest spider in the world, and it attacks birds, lizards, and frogs.

All spiders have eight legs and a body that is divided into two parts. They can sense other animals through their legs, which are very sensitive to movement.

Goliath bird-eating spiders make a hissing noise to warn predators away. If that doesn't work, they rear up on their back legs and expose their fangs, ready to bite. They can also shoot irritating hairs at attackers.

Spiders use the hairs on their legs to sense the movements of other animals that are nearby.

10.25 in. (26 cm)

Actual size!

HOW SCARY?

A Nasty Bite

The body of a goliath bird-eating spider can measure more than 4 inches (10 cm) and each fang is about 0.75 inches (2 cm) long. These spiders can inject venom when they bite.

KILLER FACT

Females can live for 20 years. Males rarely live for more than six years because they die after mating.

KILLER BEE

One bee on its own is unlikely to do much harm to a person. When a group of bees gets together, it's a different matter. A buzzing, angry swarm is terrifying—and dangerous.

Killer bees will chase an animal over longer distances than normal bees.

HOW SCARY?

BUG BITES

Length: 0.75 in. (2 cm)

Habitat: Where flowers grow

Where: South and Central America, United States

Weapons: Venomous sting

Fast Fighters

Killer bees are much more likely to attack than ordinary bees. They are quick to create huge angry swarms and can detect people 49 feet (15 m) away from their nests.

Bees feed on nectar and pollen from flowers, so they will only sting other animals or people to defend themselves from attack. Most bees have a single sting with tiny hooks called barbs on it. The barbs help the sting to stay in the victim, while venom is pumped into the victim's body, causing pain and swelling.

The sting of a killer bee is no worse than any other bee. It is only a problem when an animal is stung lots of times.

9

ASSASSIN BUG

Assassin bugs may be small, but they are deadly predators. These blood-sucking beasts hunt prey using a variety of cunning tricks.

Assassin bugs hold on to prey using sticky pads on their front legs. Needle-like mouthparts pierce the victim's body and inject a toxic liquid that turns flesh into a tasty juice. A big cockroach takes just three seconds to die—and the bug then sucks up its liquid meal.

Some assassin bugs ambush their prey, or trick them by dangling dead insects near the entrance to their homes. Others pretend to be flies caught in a web, so they can pounce on the spider that comes to investigate.

The toxic **saliva** in the bite can cause blindness.

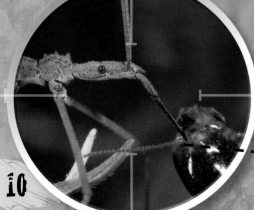

This assassin bug is attacking a termite worker.

An assassin bug's bite is one of the most painful insect bites in the world.

Kissing Bug

Kissing bugs are assassin bugs that prey on larger animals, such as mammals, birds, and people. They suck blood from their victims and pass on the deadly Chagas disease.

BUG BITES

Length: 1.6 in. (4 cm)

Habitat: Many, from yards to forests

Where: Worldwide

Weapons: Needle-sharp bite that can inject bacteria

HOW SCARY?

FUNNEL-WEB SPIDER

Funnel-web spiders have glossy, brown, or black bodies, and do not look all that scary. But looks can be deceiving ...

A funnel-web spider waits in its tunnel for a tasty treat to pass by.

BUG BITES

Length: 1.2 in. (3 cm)

Habitat: Homes, yards, and forests

Where: Southeast Australia

Weapons: Enormous fangs

HOW SCARY?

Hidden from View

Funnel web spiders hide in dark, damp places. They live in burrows and weave silken trip lines around the entrances. When a little creature walks on the silk thread, the spider feels the vibrations and leaps out of its burrow to attack.

The venom affects the **nervous systems** of humans and monkeys, but not other mammals.

KILLER FACT

Funnel-web spiders can't swim, but they can stay alive in water for up to 30 hours.

Of all funnel-web spiders, the most dangerous are male Sydney funnel-web spiders, which have such deadly venom they can kill their prey in seconds. They have fangs nearly 0.4 in. (1 cm) long.

When it is time to mate, male Sydney funnel-web spiders come out of their burrows to look for females. They search relentlessly, and attack anyone who gets in their way.

PARALYSIS TICK

Ticks are mini monsters with eight legs, like spiders, and a blood-sucking lifestyle. Most ticks cause little harm, but some of them carry a deadly secret.

These bugs are **parasites**, which means they feed on another animal while it is still alive. Ticks have sharp mouthparts that pierce a hole in a victim's flesh, and inject a liquid to stop blood from **clotting**. The ticks suck blood until their bodies are large and swollen, and then they fall to the ground.

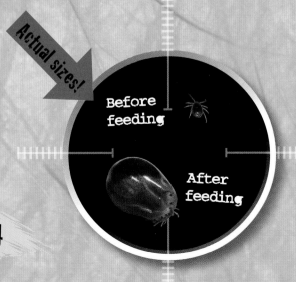

Actual sizes!

Before feeding

After feeding

Australian paralysis ticks have another nasty trick. They don't just suck blood—they inject a venom that causes the victim to become **paralyzed**. Without treatment, the victim may die.

build a
t out of
n bodies
ifferent
each day.

Numbers

ocial insects that live
ge groups called
nts have hooks on
h help them to
together to make
called bivouacs,
n bodies.

BLACK WIDOW SPIDER

Black widow spiders are known as dangerous, but it's insects that have most to fear from their venomous attacks. Black widows set traps and deliver lethal bites.

KILLER FACT

Occasionally, female black widows kill and eat males after mating with them.

The spiders add drops of glue to the threads of a web to make them more sticky.

Black widows build messy webs using special bristles on their legs. Once the victim is trapped in the web, a spider can inject it with venom that is up to 15 times stronger than that of a rattlesnake, but in much smaller amounts.

Smart Moves

Most male spiders have to impress the females before mating. A male Australian redback spends more than an hour dancing for a female, but if she doesn't like his dance, she might eat him!

Black widows only bite people to defend themselves and their bites are rarely fatal

BUG BITES

Length: 0.6 in. (15 mm)

Habitat: Warm, dark places

Where: North America

Weapons: A nasty bite, a sticky web, and strong venom

HOW SCARY?

MOSQUITO

At their best, mosquitoes are buzzing, biting bloodsuckers. At their worst, these flies are among the world's most dangerous pests.

Male mosquitoes mostly feed from flowers, but females have to feed on blood before they can lay their eggs. They search out mammals and birds to attack, and have long mouthparts that pierce skin.

The tip of the mouthpart is needle-sharp.

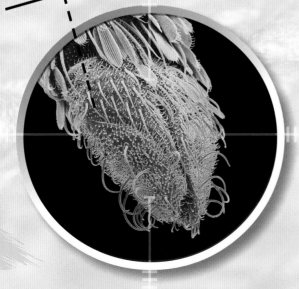

As they break the skin, mosquitoes inject saliva to stop blood from clotting so they can keep sucking it up. Mosquitoes are parasites, and the animals they feed upon are called **hosts**.

Mosquito's abdomen swells with blood.

Females find prey by detecting carbon dioxide (the gas we breathe out) and body warmth.

KILLER FACT

About 250 million people are infected with malaria every year, causing nearly one million of them to die.

Deadly Disease

Some mosquitoes, especially those that live in hot countries, carry **bacteria** that cause sickness. When the flies move from host to host, they pass on the bacteria, which can lead to deadly diseases such as malaria and dengue fever.

SCORPION

The huge imperial scorpion has powerful pincers to kill its prey. Smaller, weaker scorpions rely on venomous stings to defeat their victims.

BUG BITES

Length: 8 in. (20 cm)

Habitat: Hot, dark, and dry places

Where: Worldwide

Weapons: Powerful claws and a venom-filled stinger

HOW SCARY?

The imperial scorpion holds the record as the world's largest scorpion.

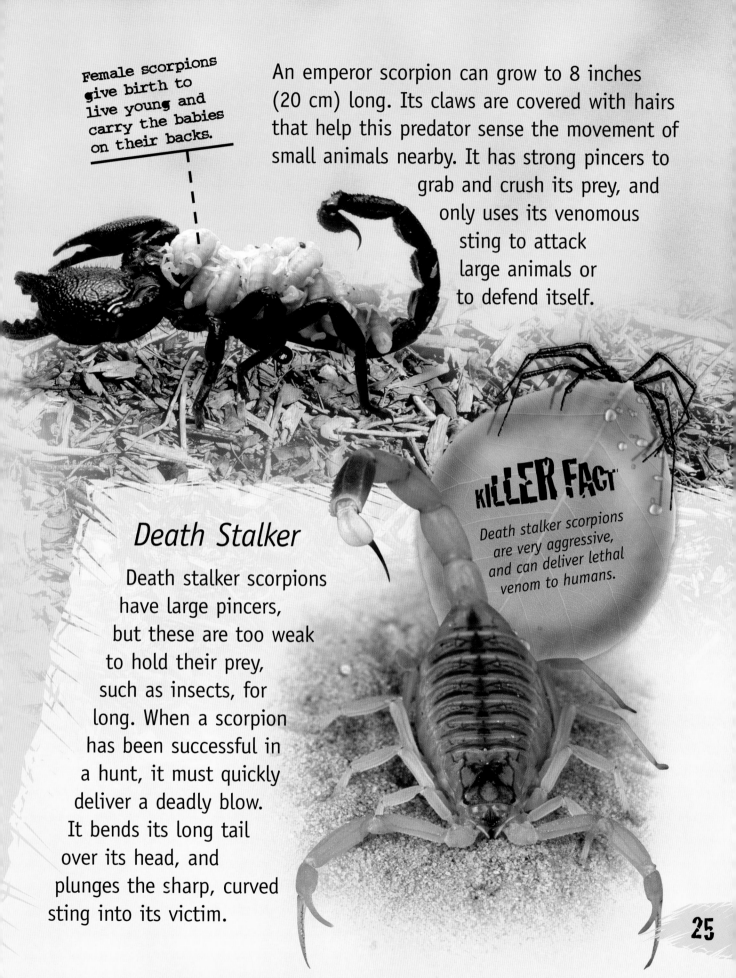

Female scorpions give birth to live young and carry the babies on their backs.

An emperor scorpion can grow to 8 inches (20 cm) long. Its claws are covered with hairs that help this predator sense the movement of small animals nearby. It has strong pincers to grab and crush its prey, and only uses its venomous sting to attack large animals or to defend itself.

Death Stalker

Death stalker scorpions have large pincers, but these are too weak to hold their prey, such as insects, for long. When a scorpion has been successful in a hunt, it must quickly deliver a deadly blow. It bends its long tail over its head, and plunges the sharp, curved sting into its victim.

KILLER FACT

Death stalker scorpions are very aggressive, and can deliver lethal venom to humans.

25

BROWN RECLUSE SPIDER

Brown recluse spiders may be small, but they are fanged, fast-moving, eight-legged predators.

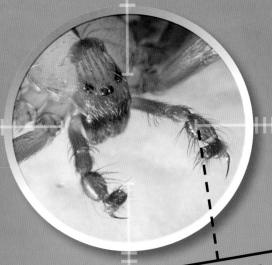

The pedipalps are short limbs on either side of the head.

Brown recluse spiders use special legs, called pedipalps, to grab and hold their prey while they inject venom with fangs. The bite of a brown recluse is usually painless to a human, but within a few hours a sore wound develops, which needs to be treated by a doctor.

KILLER FACT

Brown recluse spiders have a violin-shaped marking on their bodies, and are sometimes called violin spiders.

This spider's venom works by eating away at the skin, and can cause death in some people.

Most spiders have eight eyes, but brown recluse spiders have six. They build large, sticky webs that look like silken sheets, and often make their homes in dark corners of houses. They use their webs to hold their egg sacs, not to catch prey, which they hunt at night.

BUG BITES

Length: 0.6 in. (15 mm)

Habitat: Mostly tropical areas

Where: Worldwide

Weapons: Sharp fangs and a skin-eating venom

HOW SCARY?

27

LONOMIA

KILLER FACT

Scientists hope to be able to make life-saving medicine using lonomia venom.

A killer caterpillar's deadly spines send out a clear warning to predators—this mini monster won't make a tasty snack.

The colorful caterpillar becomes a brown moth.

A lonomia caterpillar will become a moth one day. While it is still young, however, a caterpillar's job is to eat and grow—and avoid being eaten itself.

Most caterpillars rely on camouflage to stay safe. They are often green or brown so they can hide on the plants they eat. Lonomia caterpillars, however, are covered with sharp spines that they want predators to notice!

Prickles and Poison

The sharp spines warn predators, such as birds, lizards, and frogs, that this soft-bodied mini monster is carrying a nasty venom. The spines break when they pierce a victim's skin, and the venom enters its body.

The bright colors help to warn predators.

If enough venom gets into a person's body, it can cause severe pain, bruising, and even death!

BUG BITES

Length: 2.4 in. (6 cm) long

Habitat: Rain forests

Where: South America

Weapons: Venom-tipped spines all over its body

HOW SCARY?

JUMPER ANT

There are at least 10,000 species of ant in the world. Most ants can bite or sting—or make venomous droplets that inflict pain. Their venom is similar to that of bees.

This jumper ant has managed to catch a bee in its jaws.

Bulldog and jumper ants are larger than most ants, and use their excellent eyesight to find other ants and bees to prey on. They are aggressive insects that will leap into action when they are threatened—and can actually jump at a victim!

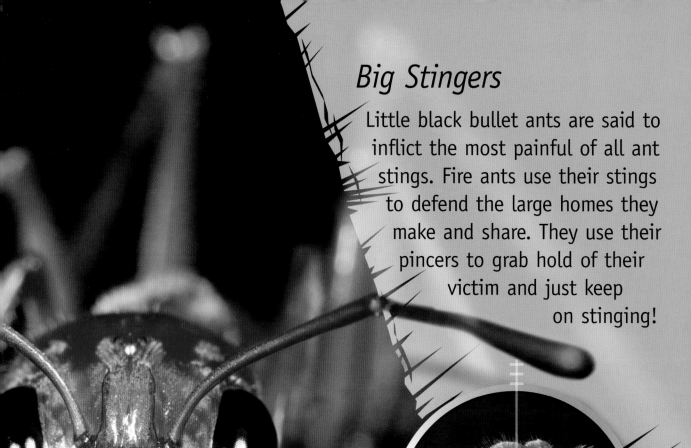

Big Stingers

Little black bullet ants are said to inflict the most painful of all ant stings. Fire ants use their stings to defend the large homes they make and share. They use their pincers to grab hold of their victim and just keep on stinging!

As jumper ants sink their large jaws into an animal or human, they use a stinger to inject powerful chemicals that cause great pain.

BUG BITES

Length: 1 in. (25 mm)

Habitat: Forests

Where: Australia

Weapons: Strong jaws and a painful stinger

HOW SCARY?

31

GLOSSARY

bacteria
Tiny life forms that are too small to see with the naked eye. Bacteria are found wherever there is life on Earth.

clotting
The process by which blood thickens after a wound has been made.

colony
A large group of animals living closely together.

hosts
Animals that parasites such as mosquitoes feed on.

invertebrates
Animals such as insects and spiders that do not have a backbone.

larvae
The young of animals such as insects, which change shape completely when they become adults.

mating
When a male and a female animal come together to reproduce.

nervous system
A network of nerve cells in an animal's body that carries signals to and from the brain.

paralyze
To stop a part of an animal's body from moving or feeling pain.

parasites
Animals or plants that feed on other animals or plants, called hosts. Parasites often cause their hosts harm.

predators
Animals that hunt other animals to eat.

prey
Animals that are hunted by predators.

saliva
A liquid made inside an animal's mouth.

segments
Parts of an animal's body that are similar to each other.

toxins
Poisonous substances made in the bodies of some animals, which the animals use to attack other animals.

venom
A kind of toxin that an animal injects into its victim's body by biting or stinging.

TAKING IT FURTHER

What makes a mini monster "scary?" Now it's time for you to decide.

- Choose some scary features (such as speed, size, habitat, number of legs, type of weapon) and special powers (such as venom or disease).

- Use this book, and the Internet, to award up to five points for each of a mini monster's scary features.

- Turn your results into a table, graph, or chart. Add up the totals to get a "Creepy Count" for each mini monster.

USEFUL WEB SITES

venomous—spiders.nanders.dk/spiderpictures.htm
Research lots more deadly spiders, in creepy close—up.

www.nationalzoo.si.edu/Audiences/kids
Enjoy animal games, books, and funny facts.

www.biology4kids.com/files/invert_main.html
Discover more invertebrates at this fact—packed web site.

kids.nationalgeographic.com/kids
A great site for exploring the natural world.

TOP **5** **DEADLY** MONSTER FACTS!

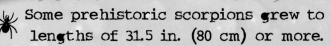

🕷 Some prehistoric scorpions grew to lengths of 31.5 in. (80 cm) or more.

🕷 The deadliest mini monsters are microscopic bugs such as bacteria that cause serious sickness.

🕷 There are an estimated 10,000,000,000,000,000 ants in the world, and most of them can bite or sting!

🕷 Bird-eating spiders shoot stinging hairs at their victims, causing intense pain.

🕷 Funnel-web spider venom is deadly to humans and monkeys, but not to most other animals.

INDEX